STAINED GLASS
in Canterbury Cathedral

SARAH BROWN

CATHEDRAL GIFTS LTD

© Cathedral Gifts Ltd 1991
Reprinted 1995

Text by Sarah Brown
Produced by Scala Publications
for Cathedral Gifts Ltd

Designed and set on Ventura in
Palatino by Roger Davies,
Green Street Press

ISBN 0 906211 31 X

Photographic Acknowledgements
Photographs on pages 1, 7,
10-11, 15, 17, 18, 22, 28, 29, 30,
31, 33, 34, 35, 36-7, 38, 39, 40,
41, 43, 44, 45, 46, 47, 48, 49, 50,
51, 52, 56, 74-5, 77, 78 © Sonia
Halliday and Laura Lushington;
2-3, 8, 12, 23, 24, 25, 57, 59, 61,
63, 65, 66, 67, 70-71, 72 © The
Royal Commission on the
Historical Monuments of
England; 26-7, 42 © Angelo
Hornak.

Frontispiece:
North Choir Aisle
The Magi warned in a dream

North Choir Aisle
Christ leading the Gentiles >

Printed and bound in Italy by
Editoriale Libraria, Trieste, Italy

RO DE RE DV XI☩

XVE SEQ VENTAS

Contents

Introduction

The stained glass and its original programme

On the 5th of September, in the year of grace 1174, about 9 0'clock, the wind blowing from the south with a fury almost beyond conception, a fire broke out . . . Thus the house of God, hitherto delightful like a paradise of pleasure, then lay contemptible in the ashes of the fire . . . The grief of the sons of the Church was so great that they howled, rather than sang Matins and Vespers . . .

Eyewitness account of Gervase, a monk of Canterbury

IT was out of this cataclysm that the splendour of Canterbury Cathedral was born. Another catastrophe, the murder in 1170 of Archbishop Thomas Becket (canonised in 1173), had given the Cathedral priory a saint of international stature and a powerful new attraction to pilgrims, who came to Canterbury in enormous numbers to make offerings, first at Becket's tomb and later at his magnificent new shrine.

It was with the proceeds from this lucrative pilgrim trade that the Christ Church community was able to rebuild the eastern arm of its church and to fill it with stained glass of extraordinary richness. Unlike the builders of York Minster, who were always short of money, the monks of Canterbury did not need to rely on a hotchpotch of donors in order to fill their windows. This building of unprecedented

<
View from the the Trinity Chapel looking into the Corona. The original shrine of St Thomas Becket stood beneath the chandelier in the present picture.

scale and complexity together with its sumptuous fittings was completed in a remarkably short space of time and the glazing scheme is unusually homogeneous in its planning and execution.

The eastern parts of the church served two distinct categories of worshipper. The medieval cathedral was also the church of a community of Benedictine monks, and in the body of the choir the monks observed the daily routine in the monastic office. The windows of this part of the church were therefore of a very different character from those in the Trinity Chapel further east, where the jewelled shrine of St Thomas was situated. It was to this part of the church that the pilgrims made their way.

The monks at their devotions could contemplate clerestory windows that depicted the genealogy of Christ as told in the Bible, a series of paired figures that began on the north side (the side of darkness) with the Creator and Adam and culminated on the south side (the side of light) with the Virgin Mary and Christ himself, the new Adam and the new Eve. Sadly these last figures have been lost, but 48 of the original 86 remain, some now relocated in the south-west transept and some in the west window. (Adam is illustrated opposite).

The clerestory series was interrupted by two rose windows which echoed the themes of light and dark, old and new. The north-east transept rose depicted at its centre Moses and Synagogia surrounded by the Prophets, representing the Old Law, while on the south side the rose window has been reconstructed, probably correctly, to show the Virgin Mary and Ecclesia (the Church), representing the New Law.

An equally biblical emphasis was to be found in the windows at aisle level, where the monks could study twelve windows containing events from both Old and New Testament, arranged to demonstrate the way in which events in the Old Testament had prefigured events in the New. This so-called typological interpretation was extremely common in the Middle Ages and was to be found in one of the most popular medieval books, the *Biblia Pauperum* or 'Poor Man's Bible'. The Canterbury typological windows are extremely sophisticated in their conception. Each New Testament event was flanked by Old Testament ones; the Adoration of the Magi and Shepherds, for example, has the Visit of the Queen of Sheba to the left and Joseph's brothers and the Egyptians before Joseph on the right. Although only a small proportion of the panels from this part of the church survive (in the north choir aisle) over 200 are described in detail in three surviving medieval manuscripts.

In the small triforium windows above the choir aisle the monks were reminded of the lives and example of two of Becket's most illustrious predecessors, Sts Dunstan and Alphege, to whom altars in the presbytery were dedicated. Dunstan, the great monastic reformer, had lived to a great age, but Alphege had died a martyr's death in 1012 at the hands of the pagan Danes.

The typological treatment of biblical scenes was continued into the Corona chapel at the far east, where the Passion of Christ and the Redemption were matched with Old Testament parallels. The chapel also contains vestiges of a splendid Tree of Jesse, in which Christ's family tree is literally depicted as a climbing vine inhabited by His royal ancestors. Although only two original panels survive, this Jesse tree is arguably one of the finest examples surviving from the late twelfth century, the equal in beauty of those from the abbey of St Denis and the Cathedral of Chartres.

Perhaps the most remarkable windows of all were those illuminating the aisles of the Trinity Chapel. Having completed a sometimes long and arduous journey, as immortalised in Chaucer's *Canterbury Tales*, the pilgrim would enter the Cathedral in eager anticipation of the splendours of St Thomas's shrine. The richly coloured glass of the aisle windows, augmented by wall and vault painting, would for many be the finest thing they would ever see, a fitting prelude to the shrine itself. As the pilgrims approached the shrine, the miraculous events associated with the saint's burial place unfolded in stained glass pictures, reminding them of the purpose of their visit.

Two detailed accounts of Becket's death and the miracles that began to take place at his tomb were written in the years immediately following the murder. Both authors (Benedict, later prior of Peterborough, and William) were Canterbury monks who would have known the saint, and the twelve miracle windows drew on these accounts of events that occurred between 1171 and 1173, emphasizing the efficacy of visiting the tomb. They depicted events that took place within the

> *West window*
Newly driven from the Garden of Eden, Adam has clothed his nakedness with an animal skin (the hooves are still attached) and is forced to labour with an iron-shod spade. Originally this figure of Adam, now positioned in the west window, accompanied one of God the Father and was the first of a series showing the Ancestors of Christ placed in the clerestory windows at the east end of the Cathedral. It dates from about 1180.

memory of many people alive at the time they were being made, between about 1200 and 1220, and show both the original tomb in the crypt beneath the Trinity Chapel and the later sumptuous shrine to which St Thomas's body was translated on 7 July 1220, in the presence of King Henry III.

The stories were chosen to show the full gamut of medieval society receiving comfort and aid from St Thomas's intercession; Louis VII, King of France, Robert of Cricklade, prior of St Frideswide's in Oxford, the boy herdsman Richard Sunieve, the child Robert of Rochester, the blind Juliana (illustrated opposite). Each scene is described in a Latin inscription that would no doubt have been unintelligble to many of the faithful. It seems likely that the monks were on hand to explain the scenes to the visitors, much as cathedral guides do today. Only seven out of the original twelve miracle windows survive, and none of the depictions of St Thomas are in original medieval glass; King Henry VIII prohibited and defaced images of St Thomas and destroyed his beautiful shrine. Further attacks on the images in these and other windows in the Cathedral took place in the 1640s, led by the puritan preacher 'Blue Dick' Culmer.

The fire of 1174 had left untouched the nave and transepts built by Archbishop Lanfranc (1070-89), but in the late fourteenth century this part of the Cathedral was also rebuilt. Demolition of the old nave began c1378, and contributors to the cost of the new work included King Richard II (1377-99). Indeed, it would seem that the generosity of individual donors was a far more important factor in the

<

North aisle

Gerard leads his blind daughter Juliana on a pilgrimage. Her eyes are shown sealed, as described in the written accounts, and she holds her father's shoulder for support

glazing of the nave than it had been in the earlier glazing of the east end. There is unfortunately no evidence for the whole scheme of nave windows, which have been almost completely swept away, but the tastes and devotions of the donors no doubt determined the contents of the windows; Archbishop Courtenay (1381-96), for example, gave £20 for a window depicting St Alphege. The two great windows that survive from this period, the west window and the north-west transept window, are both associated with Kings — Richard II and Edward IV — and reflect the royal favour enjoyed by Canterbury during the late Middle Ages. Both the Black Prince, Richard's father, and King Henry IV, Richard's successor, chose to be buried not in Westminster Abbey, but near the shrine of St Thomas in the Trinity Chapel of Canterbury Cathedral.

The west window which stands above the principal entrance to the nave was glazed either by or in honour of King Richard II, and his arms, together with those of both of his wives, appear in the apex of the window. The King's heraldry was accompanied by small figures of apostles and prophets, 28 of which survive. The original conception of the window is now rather confused by the insertion, already mentioned, of a number of early figures of Christ's ancestors from the genealogical series designed for the east end, but the main subject was originally a series of English kings including Canute, Edward the Confessor and William the Conqueror. Eight of the kings survive, but without their identifying inscriptions, already heavily patched in the eighteenth century when some of them could still be deciphered. Such a gallery of royal figures would have seemed most appropriate for the window over the door by which a visiting monarch would enter the Cathedral.

The kings are painted in a very different style from the early figures against which

<

The Corona
The Ascension from the
Redemption Window in the
Corona.

> *West window*
> The arms of King Richard II occupy the apex of the west window. A lifelong devotion to his illustrious predecessor St Edward the Confessor led Richard to adopt the impaled arms seen here: the coat with a cross and five martlets was Edward the Confessor's. The arms of both of Richard's wives, Anne of Bohemia and Isabella of France, also appear. Although the exact nature of Richard's involvement in this commission is not clear he is known to have contributed to the cost of the completion of the nave, and may well have contributed also to the cost of the window, with its strong royal subject matter. It seems likely that the window dates from before Richard's deposition in 1399.

they can now so easily be compared. The strongly linear strokes of the twelfth and thirteenth century glass-painters have given way to a softer, more highly modelled and naturalistic style. The kings stare out of the window with grave expressions, recalling the heavy burdens of kingship.

The second window with a royal association is the great window filling the north-west transept, often called the Royal Window. Dating from the 1480s, the window preserves the kneeling figures of King Edward IV, his queen, Elizabeth Woodville, together with their two surviving sons and five surviving daughters. The King and Queen had lost a further two daughters and a son in infancy. The boys are known to history as the Princes in the Tower, whence they were taken in June 1483, after their father's death, and murdered in mysterious circumstances. Edward's eldest daughter, Elizabeth, also depicted in this window, later became Queen of England as the wife of Henry VII and appears with him in glass in the chapel of Christ's College, Cambridge.

The Royal Window, which overlooks the place of Becket's martyrdom, was the major victim of Culmer's vandalism in the 1640s and it is from his gleeful account of the destruction that we know that above the royal figures there were once scenes of the Crucifixion and the Joys of the Virgin, together with life-size figures of the Virgin and St Thomas Becket. Culmer particularly enjoyed climbing the city ladder and 'ratling down proud Becket's glassy bones' with a pike.

The portraits of the King and his family are vivid in their evocation of medieval royalty. The family kneel before carved prayer desks in front of beautiful hangings decorated with heraldic motifs. The queen wears a crucifix on a chain at her belt. The glass-painters have achieved a degree of realism in their painting which suggests familiarity with Flemish panel-painting of the period. Indeed the glass portraits may well have been based on panel portraits painted from life; a portrait of Elizabeth Woodville attributed to John Stratford in Queen's College, Cambridge, provides a remarkable comparison with the glass. The serenity of this family portrait belies the tragedy that was soon to befall them.

For its quality, its diversity and its sheer splendour, the stained glass of the Cathedral is justifiably recognised as one of its great treasures.

∨

Rose Window
Late twelfth-century representation of Moses and Synagogia.

Post-Medieval Stained Glass

anterbury's rich heritage of medieval stained glass cannot really be matched by later windows, but there are a number of important twentieth-century ones that should be included in any stained glass itinerary of the Cathedral.

All but eight of the original medieval figures made for the choir clerestory were removed in the eighteenth century — they can now be seen in the west window and south-west transept. Many of the medieval foliage borders and all of the metal armatures remained, however, and from 1861 to 1862 these windows were filled with a remarkable series of figures of Christ's ancestors faithfully copied by George Austin from the surviving originals. All but four of these figures were destroyed in the air raids of 1942, but in the 1950s equally impressive new copies were made by Samuel Caldwell. The figures, striking examples of the modern glazier's skill, have helped to recreate the rich and glowing atmosphere of the medieval choir. Austin's work survives in the impressive south rose window and in St John's and St Gregory's Chapels.

Another casualty of the 1942 raids was a pair of windows made in 1900 for St Andrew's Chapel by the outstanding Arts and Crafts artist Christopher Whall. Fortunately, a third Whall window of 1902 survives in the west wall of the south-west transept. It depicts the Nativity, the Agony in the Garden and the Resurrection. Its rich, jewel-like colours reflect Whall's reverence for medieval glass, which he had studied widely — indeed, he incorporated fifteenth-century fragments in the tracery lights. Facing Whall's window in the

Chapel of St Michael, or Warriors Chapel, is a window dedicated to the Buffs, the East Kent Regiment. Dating from 1959, this fine heraldic window is the work of the Edinburgh artist William Wilson. The coats of arms are those of the colonels of the regiment from 1665 to 1957. In a church with so much medieval heraldic glass, it is fascinating to see heraldry so successfully expressed in a modern form. The archangels in the other window are by the London firm of Clayton and Bell (c1906), whose work can also be seen at the east end of the nave north aisle (c1881) and west wall of the north-east transept (c1867).

Whall, who designed his first windows in 1880, was the most influential of the stained glass artists working according to the Arts and Crafts philosophy generated by William Morris. In order to keep complete control over his work, Whall taught himself every aspect of the stained glass craft, believing that the limitations of the medium was also its 'chief opportunity'. In 1889, the invention of Prior's 'Early English Slab' glass provided him with the material that was to stimulate his creativity and was to become the hallmark of his work. The glass is of a thick and uneven texture which serves to intensify light and colour. The jewel-like effects that Whall sought were further enhanced by his generous use of pure white glass, which emphasizes the richness of the colour and gives his windows their sparkling quality. His Canterbury window is one of the most successful and sympathetic post-medieval contributions to the Cathedral's glazing.

A window in a very different mould can be seen in the west wall of the opposite

^

South-east transept

The themes of the south-east transept windows, Peace (left) and Salvation (right), must have seemed particularly appropriate to Ervin Bossanyi who had himself fled from intolerance and oppression in 1930s. In his 1958 Salvation window Christ frees the captive from a prison which has the Nazi swastika as its keyhole.

transept. The work mostly of J. Ninian Comper (1864-1960), the window is in the historicist tradition of the Victorian firms exemplified by that of Charles Eamer Kempe whose work was strongly influenced by the pictorial style of the fifteenth and early sixteenth centuries, using large quantities of white glass, yellow stain. Retaining fragments of its 1470s glazing, the gift of John Barnewell and the Salt Fishmongers of London and some remnants of another window destroyed in

∧
Chapter House : West Window
Lanfranc plans the new Cathedral

<
South-west transept
Christopher Whall window

Window' of the 1480s with its portraits of Edward IV and his family, although its rather pallid colours undermine its impact.

It is in the south-east transept that the most dramatically modern windows in the Cathedral are to be found. In 1956 a window with a theme most appropriate to the era, God the Father of all Races, was installed, the first of four by the Hungarian artist Ervin Bossanyi, a refugee from Fascism who came to England in the 1930s. He drew upon the folk art of his homeland for inspiration; the naive, wide-eyed, almost child-like figures belie the sophistication and consummate craftsmanship of this artist. In St Anselm's Chapel, to the east of Bossanyi's windows, is a work by another twentieth-century glass-painter, better known in his native York. Harry Stammers' vividly coloured figures of 1959 portray St Anselm himself accompanied by his predecessor Lanfranc, his physician Baldwin and Kings William Rufus and Henry I. Anselm holds a copy of his great treatise on the Incarnation, *Cur Deus Homo*, his most famous and important work.

There is also stained glass to be seen outside the main body of the cathedral church. To the north of the nave is the cloister and the Chapter House. The cloister contains work by followers of Comper, whose window in the north-west transept has already been described. In the east walk, Christopher Webb's window of c1934 depicts St Gregory the Great, the author of the papal mission to the Anglo-Saxons accompanied by the first four archbishops of Canterbury — Augustine, Laurentius, Mellitus and Justus. In the west walk are two windows with tracery lights filled by Hugh Easton, perhaps best known as the author of the Royal Air Force memorial window in Westminster Abbey. From c1934 are the musicians Henry Purcell, John Marbeke, Thomas Tallis and Archbishop Stephen Langton, while the

1942, by the Victorian firm of Ward and Hughes the window is now a memorial to King George VI and a commemoration of the Coronation of Queen Elizabeth II. It was installed in 1954, the gift of the Freemasons of Kent, and depicts in its lower register King George, Queen Elizabeth (now the Queen Mother) and the Princesses Elizabeth and Margaret, with the figures of Queen Elizabeth, the Duke of Edinburgh and their children, flanked by dignitaries of Church and State present at the Coronation above. In its realistic portrait of the royal family, the window is similar in spirit to the adjoining 'Royal

^

North-west transept
The Royal Family by Sir Ninian Comper given by the Freemasons of Kent, 1954.

1939 window in memory of Dean Richard Lawrie Sheppard illustrates the Adoration of the Shepherds, a pelican in her piety, St Francis and St Martin. The dean appears in the guise of one of the adoring shepherds, in a play on his own name. The scheme to fill all of the cloister windows with stained glass was never realised, but being at ground level, they can be studied with greater ease than some of those inside the church.

On the eastern side of the cloister is the entrance to the fourteenth-century Chapter House, dominated by two large windows which were filled at the turn of the century by the firm of Hemmings. Of historical rather than artistic interest, the east window, installed in 1896, depicts English monarchs and the archbishops of Canterbury from Queen Bertha and St Augustine in the sixth century, to Queen Victoria, who celebrated her Jubilee the year after the window was put in place, and Archbishop Benson (1883-97). The west window of 1903 contains a rich heraldic display. Thus the history of the Cathedral presides over the building in which so much of its day-to-day business has been transacted.

A GUIDE TO
THE WINDOWS

THE following section of this book is designed to act as a guide around the Cathedral to the most important and beautiful glass. It follows the same route as the official tour. All of the best glass is illustrated and the main windows (West Window, North-West Transept, South-West Transept, Biblia Pauperum I and II, St Alphege and St Dunstan, North-East Transept, Trinity Chapel, Corona) are detailed. Small line plans accompany the details to help indicate where they are positioned in the main windows.

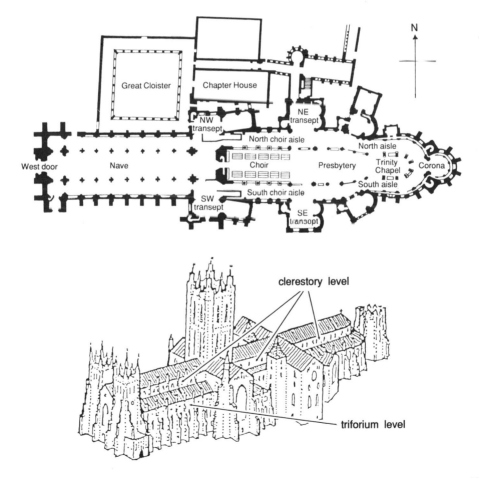

WEST WINDOW

The west window now contains a mixture of original late fourteenth-century glass and together with late twelfth-/early thirteenth-century Ancestors of Christ, removed from the choir clerestory in the eighteenth century. The Tracery lights contain fourteenth-century shields of arms and figures of Apostles. Contents of the main lights are described left to right, from top to bottom:

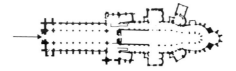

King of England (Canute?), **William the Conqueror**, **King of England** (Harold II?), **Edward the Confessor**, **King of England** (William II?), **King of England** (Henry I?), **King of England** (Stephen?), all late fourteenth century

>

Late fourteenth-century shields of arms

>

Late fourteenth-century Apostles

>

Jechonias(?), **Obed** (OBETH), **Rehoboam** (ROBOAS), all twelfth century; **King of England**, late fourteenth century (restored); **Abia** (ABIAS), **Jesse** (IESSE), all late twelfth/early thirteenth century

>

Late fourteenth-century shields of arms

>

Esrom (ESROM), **Naason** (NAASON); **Semei** (labelled SETH); **Adam** (ADAM), **Joseph** (IOSEPH), **Aminadab** (defective scroll), **Aram** (ARAN), all late twelfth/early thirteenth century

>

Late fourteenth-century royal shields of arms

>

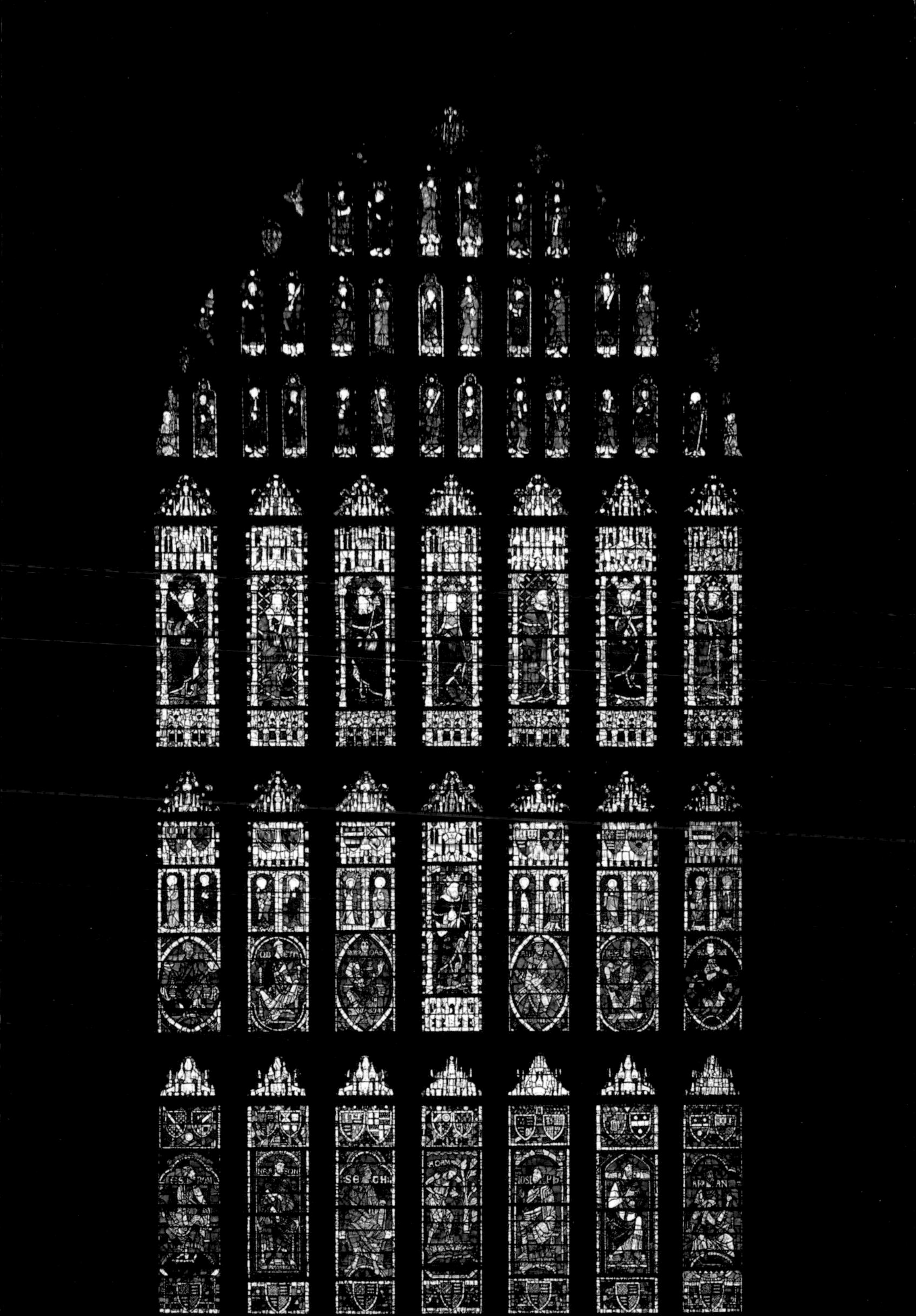

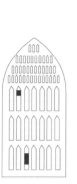

A king of England

Set against their opulent backgrounds, in imitation of damask hangings, the gallery of kings that dominated the west window would have been an impressive sight in the nave of the Cathedral in the late fourteenth century. This king is unidentified; the original inscriptions for each had mostly been lost by the eighteenth century. However, even in their present condition, these grave figures are a powerful expression of the medieval concept of kingship and would no doubt have appealed to the insecure Richard II. A gallery of kings at the west end of a cathedral had many precedents both in England and in France, although such kings were more commonly depicted in sculpture, as at the Cathedrals of Wells, Lincoln and Exeter.

Seth

The figure of Semei (labelled Seth), is the only one of the late twelfth-century genealogical figures to have a profile head, probably copied from a late Roman coin. The head, like the restored scroll, was, in fact, replaced in the nineteenth century. The original head turned up in a Rochester antique shop, and was given to the Victoria and Albert Museum in London in 1920.

<

Naason

One more in the late twelfth-century series of the Ancestors of Christ now preserved in the west window, Naason was designed to be seated below Aminadab, and his canopy formed a plinth for Aminadab above. The fine lettering used for the scroll bearing his name is typical of the elegant and legible scripts used throughout the early glass at Canterbury.

>

Aminadab

Aminadab was another of Christ's Ancestors, as recorded in the Gospel of St Matthew; like Adam, this figure in the west window was originally placed in the east end. Seated in majestic, stern pose, he is dressed in robes reminiscent of a classical statue. The head demonstrates the glazier's skill both in cutting glass in the intricate shape of the face and in leading it into position so that the lead *calmes* (strips) holding the panel together are absorbed into the outline of the design.

WEST WINDOW

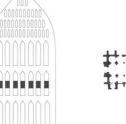

The family of King Edward IV

The 'royal window' in the north-west transept contains a striking portrait of the family of King Edward IV and his Queen Elizabeth (Woodville). Identification of the children depicted enables the window to be dated to the early 1480s, not long before the death of the King in 1483. The children include the young Edward V and his brother Richard who were immediately on their father's death imprisoned in the Tower, where they were probably murdered. In 1484 all Edward's children by Elizabeth Woodville were declared illegitimate by an Act of Parliament and their uncle Richard, Duke of Gloucester, accepted the throne to become Richard III. There were once also religious subjects in this window, including pictures of the Virgin Mary and St Thomas Becket, but they were broken out in the seventeenth century by the puritan zealot Richard ('Blue Dick') Culmer.

Elizabeth Woodville
In 1464 the young Edward IV secretly married Lady Elizabeth Woodville, daughter of Richard Woodville, Earl Rivers and widow of Sir John Grey. Edward's decision to marry an English noblewoman rather than a foreign princess, together with the subsequent advancement of his wife's family, certainly contributed to his political difficulties.

Regina Elizabetha consors
Edwardi dei gracia Regis

The Three Princesses
The princesses
Anne, Catherine and
Bridget depicted
here (the inscription
naming Elizabeth
and Cecily is an
eighteenth-century
restoration) had lost
two sisters (Mary
and Margaret) and a
brother (George) by
the time this win-
dow was created.
They were soon to
lose a father and two
more brothers. All
five of the surviving
princesses were to
share their mother's
exile.

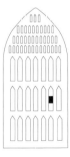

<
Methusaleh
This powerful figure of Methusaleh, famed in the Old Testament for his great age, is depicted in pensive pose indicative of his enormous wisdom. The anonymous painter responsible is now known as the 'Methusaleh Master' after this, one his most vigorous figures.

>
Whall Window: The Nativity
In 1905 Christopher Whall advised students of stained glass 'never imitate, but graft your own work onto the old, reverently . . . have also a living tradition, springing from mastery of craft – naturally, spontaneously'. That he practiced what he preached is illustrated in his own beautifully crafted work shown here on the far right.

BIBLIA PAUPERUM I
WINDOW

This window now contains panels from two separate windows. Those marked † originated here in the late twelfth century, while those marked ‡ originated in the north-east transept. They are described top to bottom, left to right.

Balaam and his Ass †, The ride of the Magi †, Isaiah and Jerusalem †

>

The Exodus†, Magi before Herod †, Christ leading the Gentiles from idolatory †

>

Solomon and the Queen of Sheba †, The adoration of the Christ Child †, Joseph and his brethren †

>

Lot's escape from Sodom †, The dream of the Magi †, Jeroboam's sacrifice †

>

Eli receiving Samuel †, The Presentation in the Temple †, The Parable of the Sower (1) ‡

>

The Church and the three sons of Noah ‡, Christ abandoned by the Pharisees ‡, The three blameless states of Life (Virginity, Continence and Marriage) ‡

>

The deceitfulness of Riches ‡, The Parable of the Sower (2) ‡, The Good Ground (personified by Job, Daniel and Noah) ‡

>

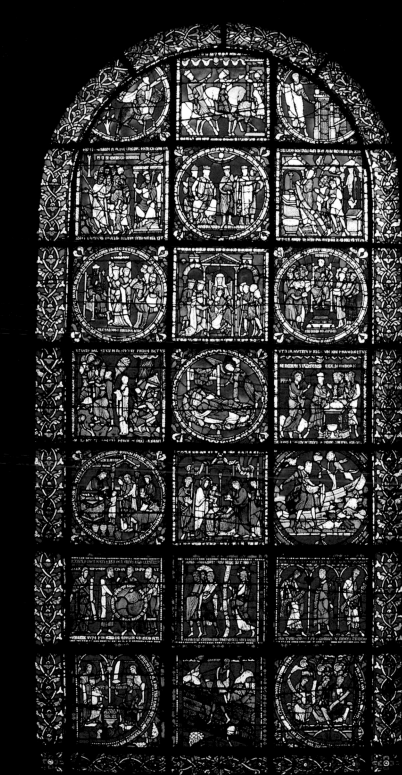

∧

The Three Magi riding

This dramatic scene from the north choir aisle windows shows the Three Magi led by the star to Bethlehem. A sense of movement and urgency is conveyed by the posture of the figures in the saddle, while the horses are depicted with more solemnity. The dappling of their flanks has been achieved by painting on both sides of the glass; its thickness and uneven texture give it its special quality.

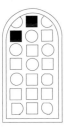

>

Exodus

This scene compresses many elements of the biblical narrative of the Exodus from Egypt of the Jews under Moses into a single crowded and lively panel. Pharoah, seated under a canopy, raises his hand in command, but clearly relies on the advice of his counsellor who stands at his side. The Israelites, led by Moses carrying a staff, head into the wilderness, guided by a column of fire, while at their feet are the waves of the Red Sea that was to be miraculously parted to let them pass, closing over the heads of the treacherous Egyptians, following in pursuit.

ERVM PLNA POPLVS: DVCENTE COLVMPDA

RT SE QVEHS CO LVMPHAM

PHARAO REX EGIPTI:G

ᴚ RE DV XI⊂

SEᑫ VE NTᴬS

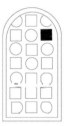

Christ leading the Gentiles
This unusual and imaginative
scene in the north choir aisle
shows Christ leading the Gentiles away from their pagan
gods. The Gentiles turn their
backs on a nude, horned
statue, while a demon fruit-
lessly attempts to turn them
back to their idolatry. Depict-
ion of the naked human body
in Romanesque art is rare, and
it is likely that surviving late
Roman sculpture provided the
inspiration for this nude to the
Canterbury glass-painters.

^
Solomon and the Queen of Sheba
This Old Testament episode was regarded as a prefiguration of the Adoration of the Christ Child by the Magi. The exotic Queen is accompanied by a retinue of Nubian riders mounted on camels: the beasts are most convincingly painted, although knowledge of them would have been only second-hand; the glaziers may have seen a picture in a bestiary or may even have heard the creatures described by a pilgrim who had returned from the east.

The Magi warned in a dream

This delightful scene in which the weary Magi rather uncomfortably share a single bed (but at least they keep warm) shows them warned in a dream not to return to Herod with news of the whereabouts of the Christ Child. The message is written on a scroll held by the angel.

<

Lot's escape from Sodom
At the destruction of Sodom
and Gomorrah, Lot's wife,
ignoring the angels' warning,
turned back for a last look at
the cities of the plains and
became a pillar of salt. The
incident was interpreted as
an antetype of the Magi
warned in a dream by the
angel.

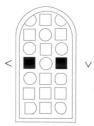

>

King Jeroboam's sacrifice
This almost perfectly preserved scene depicts King
Jeroboam making a sacrifice
at his altar at Bethel. The
prophet who approaches
from the left is advised by a
heavenly message to evade
the vengeful King by return-
ing home by another route.
This scene is the companion
to that of Lot's wife, another
antetype of the Magi
warned in a dream.

∧

Noah's sons divide the world

According to the Book of Genesis 9, 19, the whole world was repopulated after the Flood by the three sons of Noah — Ham, Shem and Japhet. Here the three are shown dividing between them a great disc representing the Earth. God's approval is indicated by the presiding figure of Ecclesia (the Church), who stands to the left.

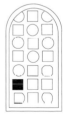

<

The Sower on good ground and among thorns
One of two scenes devoted to the Parable of the Sower, this panel was made for a window in the north-east transept but is now inserted in the north choir aisle. Both Sower scenes combine two elements from the Parable in a single composition. A landscape is effectively suggested by the diagonal strips of colour at the Sower's feet. His discarded robe lies in the foreground.

∨

The Three Righteous Men of the Old Testament
Job, Daniel and Noah, the three righteous men of the Old Testament, receive crowns from the hands of angels. As personifications of the good ground in which the word of God took hold and flourished, they were positioned to the left of the Sower (*see opposite*), representing Christ, on whom they turn their gaze.

BIBLIA PAUPERUM II WINDOW

This window contains panels from three separate typological windows. Only those marked † are original; the related panels from elsewhere are identified by ‡.

Christ among the Doctors†

Moses and Jethro†   **Daniel among the Elders†**

The Miracle of Cana‡

The Six Ages of the World‡   **The Six Ages of Man‡**

The Miraculous Draught of Fishes‡

Noah in the Ark   **St Peter preaching to the converts‡**

The calling of Nathaniel‡

The Gentiles‡   **The Pharisees‡**

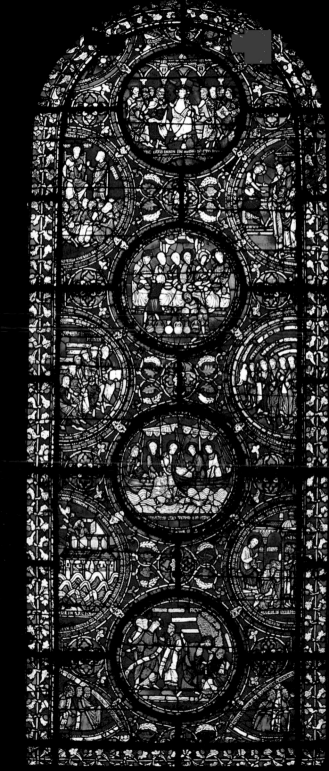

Miraculous draught of fishes
This lively scene, designed to be paired with depictions of Paul converting the Gentiles (lost) and Peter preaching to the Jews, is rarely represented in stained glass. Some of the fish are shown escaping the net of Christ's message of redemption.

Six Ages of the World
The Six Ages of the World, likened by St Augustine to the six water pots miraculously filled with wine by Christ at the marriage at Cana, are represented here by biblical figures. Each is clearly identified; Adam (with hoe), Noah (with ark), Abraham (with flame), David (with harp), Jechonias (with crown and sceptre) and Christ (with open book).

∧
Six Ages of Man
The second 'type' designed to
accompany the Miracle of Cana
and providing a counterbalance
to the Six Ages of the World,
illustrates the Six Ages of Man;
Infancy, Childhood, Adoles-
cence, Middle Age, Maturity and
Old Age.

^
Story of St Alphege: the siege of Canterbury
The legend of St Alphege is represented in late twelfth-century glass medallions in the triforium of the north choir aisle. In 1011 the pagan Danes brought their fleet to Sandwich and laid siege to the city of Canterbury. The city eventually fell to the attackers through the treachery of the Anglo-Saxon Archdeacon Aelfmaer, and Archbishop Alphege was taken prisoner.

V
St Alphege taken aboard ship

Archbishop Alphege was amongst those held hostage by the Danes. He was
held for seven months and the then enormous ransom of £3000 was demanded.
St Alphege, however, refused to allow it to be paid, and after drunken feasting
the enraged Danes slew him by hurling at him the bones of an ox. His body was
eventually buried in Canterbury where he was venerated as the Cathedral's first
martyr.

∧
St Dunstan and the miracle of Calne
Dunstan is depicted at the conference of Calne, called by his opponents, the Scottish bishops. The meeting took place in an upper room and as his adversaries voiced their criticism, the floor gave way, leaving only Dunstan and his companions unharmed.

<
St Dunstan transported by an angel
St Dunstan (908-88) is honoured in two triforium windows. This scene concerns his early life at Glastonbury, when he was prevented from entering the church to pray by a demon. Climbing to the roof, he was miraculously borne down to the altar by an angel.

NORTH-EAST ROSE WINDOW

Moses and Synagogia are surrounded by crowned female figures representing the four cardinal virtues — Justice, Temperance, Fortitude and Prudence.

∨

Rose window

Although most of the window consists of modern copies of glass now lost, these copies reproduce something of the original effect, and in their midst is a genuine late twelfth- century representation of Moses and Synagogia. Moses holds the tablets of the Old Law while Synagogia personifies the Temple before the Church. The panels of glass are held in position by metal armatures that span the width of the oculus opening; this kind of circular opening with a metal frame is very rare. By the eighteenth century, the corresponding rose window of the south-east transept was 'almost plain', but would no doubt originally have contained Christ and Ecclesia at its core, matching Moses and Synagogia here; it was restored thus in the nineteenth century.

TRINITY CHAPEL WINDOWS

Looking from the Choir towards the Trinity Chapel, which begins at the St Augustine Chair, and Corona at the furthest end. This was the work of William the Englishman, who in 1179 replaced the original architect, William of Sens, who was severely injured in a fall from the scaffolding. As the home of St Thomas's sumptuous new shrine, the Trinity Chapel was the most important part of the new church, and its slender proportions, vaulted roof, marble shafts and profusely carved capitals are in the Gothic style. Although not the first English building to embrace the new style, Canterbury's enormous prestige was to ensure its rapid and widespread acceptance throughout the country.

The windows in this part of the Cathedral show the miracles of healing brought about by St Thomas Becket. They were positioned in the Trinity Chapel so the pilgrims would see them as they approached St Thomas's shrine. Based on two detailed contemporary accounts of St Thomas's death and the subsequent miracles, the windows should be read around the north aisle and then around the south aisle of the chapel. The panels should be looked at from top to bottom. Though much of the glass has been restored these windows are some of the finest medieval stained glass in England. The panels illustrated in this section are representative of the finest work.

NATE SORTE PARI PERE G
REVE NIVN MEDICAR

> *The cure of Robert of Cricklade*
Although there are numerous cures of lameness in the Becket miracle stores, most modern authors have identified the man helped to St Thomas's tomb in this scene as Robert of Cricklade, Prior of St Frideswide's (now Christ Church) in Oxford. A letter from Robert himself was transcribed in one of the accounts of the miracles. Having prayed at the tomb in the crypt, Robert recovered on his journey home from Canterbury.

< *The daughters of Godbold of Boxley*
This is a scene showing two crippled sisters; the daughters of one Godbold of Boxley, on their laborious pilgrimage to Canterbury. First one and then the other sister witnessed a vision of St Thomas and was healed.

HIC CRVOR EST TACTVS NONDVM LANG VCR AB ACTVS

∧
The cure of Juliana of Rochester
At the tomb of St Thomas, Juliana's eyes are sponged with some of St Thomas's blood. Her cure was not immediate; she left the tomb as she had come, sightless, but her vision was restored during her homeward journey.

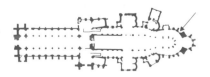

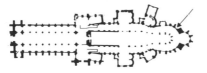

The cure of Richard Sunieve: Sunieve asleep
Six scenes in all are devoted to the story of the boy herdsman, Richard Sunieve.
He was commanded to drive out to pasture the horses of his master, Richard
Fitz Henry. Having found good grazing for the beasts, the boy took a nap and
awoke to find that he had 'leprosy'.

ONH IBARI GCTVSVIXSICAMA TRፍ REFI CIVS

∧
The cure of Richard Sunieve: the miracle
Richard was miraculously restored to health at the tomb of St Thomas. Here, in the company of his mother, he demonstrates his cure to his master, who touches his restored skin in wonderment.

<
The cure of Richard Sunieve: Sunieve the leper
The afflicted boy sits up in bed to receive a tray of food served at arm's length by his timid mother who has swathed her face in a shawl before daring to enter the room. Many kinds of skin disease were identified as leprosy in the Middle Ages, and all were feared by the healthy

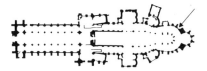

∨

The boy saved from drowning

The miracle stories recount two similar tales of children revived after drowning by the intercession of St Thomas, and here the Canterbury glass-painters have combined elements from both. The boys are seen here stoning frogs on the banks of the river Medway. One of their company has fallen into the icy-looking water.

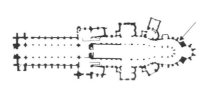

VIN ƆIC ꞇEMO LES.ꝺOM VS E G ꝟA.ꞁMOꝚ ꞁV APꝚOLES:

^

A Plague in the House of Sir Jordan Fitz Eisulf

Jordan Fitz Eisulf was a knight who had known Becket personally. When plague killed his son, it was water from St Thomas's tomb that revived him. Sir Jordan vowed to make an offering at the tomb in thanksgiving, but failed to do so even when reminded of the debt by a blind and lame beggar who had experienced a vision of the saint. In retribution for the broken vow, a further visitation of plague afflicted the household, killing the elder son. Sir Jordan finally made good his vow. The figure of the vengeful St Thomas is, like all depictions of him in the Cathedral, a modern restoration; the medieval ones were destroyed either during the Reformation or in the mid-seventeenth century.

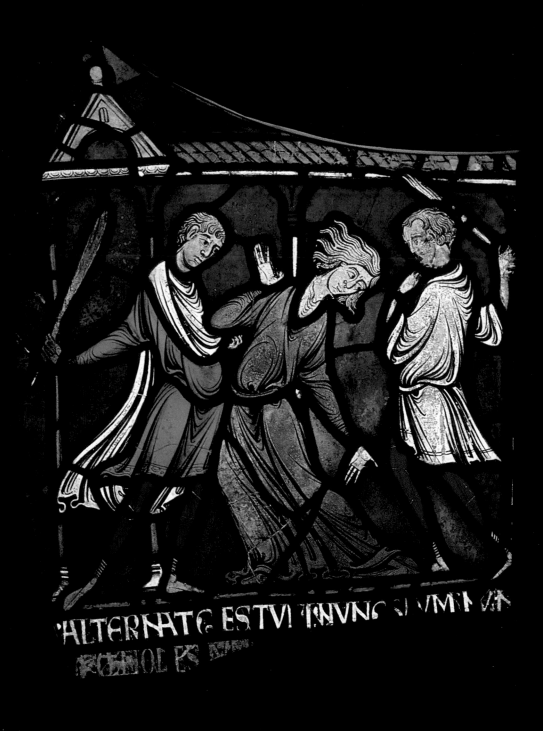

ALTERNATG EST VI TNVNG SVMI VN

<

Mathilda of Cologne

Mathilda was a mad woman of Cologne, who had committed murder. In one of her sane moments she received a vision of St Thomas and embarked on a pilgrimage to Canterbury. The medieval attitude to mental instability is displayed here, as Mathilda is subdued during one of her violent bouts by two stout attendants.

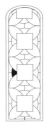

∨

Cure of Brother Elias

Elias, a monk of Reading, suffered from leprosy so severely that every morning his bed was found to be full of flakes of skin. He reveals his _affliction by pulling up his habit to uncover his arms and legs. One of the attendant physicians examines a flask of urine, a common medieval diagnostic technique.

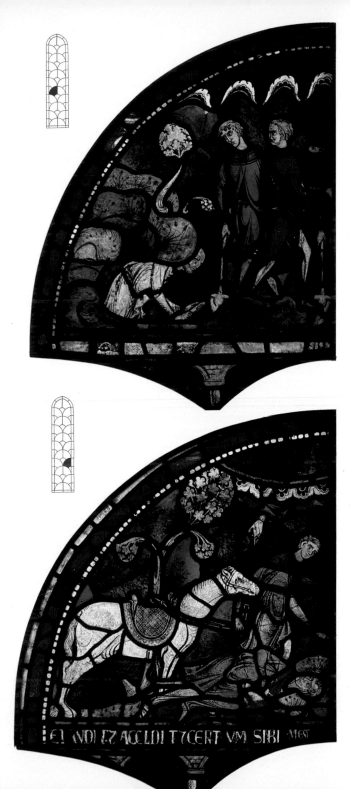

<

William of Gloucester 1
This excellently preserved
panel is one of six depicting
the fate of William of Gloucester, a contractor employed by
Roger of Pont l'Eveque, Archbishop of York. While laying
water pipes on the arch-
bishop's estate at Church-
down, William was buried by
a fall of earth.

<

William of Gloucester 2
Although his companions
were convinced of his death,
St Thomas warned a woman
in a vision that William still
lived. In this scene the archbishop's bailiff listens for
signs of life beneath the
earth and hears William's
groans. Subsequent scenes
show his deliverance.

> *Geoffrey of Winchester*
> The infant Geoffrey of Winchester had been miraculously cured of the fever by St Thomas. His mother's joy was shortlived, however, for his cradle was buried in the collapse of the house. The baby's head is clearly visible in the rubble.

> *Geoffrey of Winchester 2*
> The swooning, distraught mother calls upon St Thomas for help, while, on the left, men with pickaxes struggle to clear the debris. The child was recovered safe and sound and smiling.

CORONA
WINDOWS

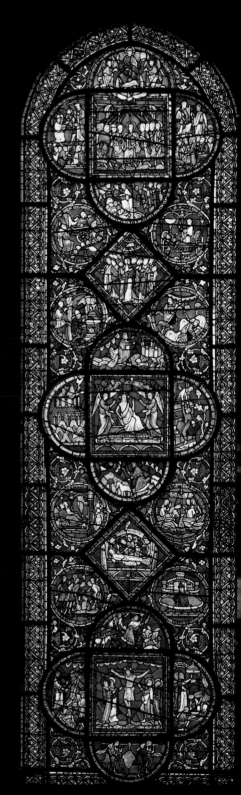

CORONA EAST WINDOW (*right*). The theme of this early thirteenth-century window is the Redemption, which unfolds in a series of 'types' and 'antetypes' linking Old and New Testament events. It is designed to be read from bottom to top. Each scene from Christ's Passion is surrounded by four Old Testament antecedents. Described in clockwise order, from bottom to top except for the apex scenes which encircle the figure of Christ in Majesty:

The Crucifixion (mostly modern); Moses striking the Rock, the offering of Isaac, The Passover, the Grapes of Eschol

The Entombment; Joseph in the Pit, Samson and Delilah, Jonah thrown into the sea, Daniel in Babylon

The Resurrection (mostly modern); Noah in the ark (modern except for the title), Michael and David (modern), Moses and the Burning Bush

The Ascension; The High Priest enters the Holy of Holies, Elijah's ascension, Isiah before Hezekiah, the translation of Enoch

Christ in Majesty and Pentecost; (anticlockwise) the consecration of Aaron and his sons, Moses and Jethro, Moses receiving the Law

ERE·ISRAHEL IGHORAT CRI STVM AGENTILISADORAT

∧

Pentecost

Near the apex of the Corona east window, this thirteenth–century panel depicts the events of Pentecost: the Holy Spirit, in the form of tongues of fire, streams down on to the heads of the apostles (reduced, after the loss of Judas, to eleven).

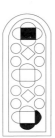

>

Preparations for Passover

The Passover is the most obvious precursor of the Passion of Christ. In this window in the Corona Chapel the enslaved and exiled Israelites paint the Tau sign on their lintels so that the Angel of Death will pass over their homes. In the foreground a lamb is sacrificed for its blood with which the sign is painted, a reminder of the sacrifice of the Paschal lamb.

The Grapes of Eschol (*previous page*)

This lunette in the Corona Chapel is one of those flanking the Crucifixion. The spies sent by Moses into Eschol in the land of Canaan return laden with grapes, evidence of the riches that lay before the Israelites in the Promised Land. The grapes, fruit of the vine, were interpreted as prefiguring the wine of the Eucharist.

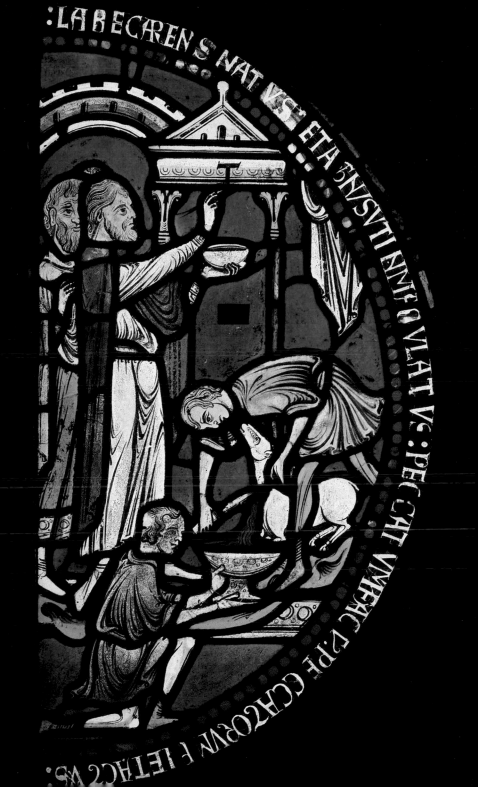

>

The Tree of Jesse - Virgin Mary and King Josias

Two figures survive from what must have been one of the love-liest Jesse Trees in European art of its date (*c*1200). The tree was a popular means of showing Christ's forebears, giving particular honour to the Virgin Mary, through whom Christ was descended from the House of David. She is here accompanied by King Josias. David, Solomon and a recumbent figure of Jesse, from whose body the tree would have sprung, would certainly have been included, but have all been lost. Jesse Trees are common in both twelfth- and thirteenth-century windows, and other examples survive in York and Salisbury in England and in St Denis, Chartres, Soissons, Troyes and the Ste Chapelle in Paris in France.

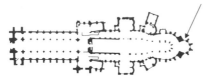

IOS IAS

Conservation and Restoration

STAINED glass has always fascinated people because of its bright and vivid colours illuminated by the sunlight. Therefore it is astonishing that medieval glass consists mainly of sand and beech ash. However, just these main components have been and are decisive for the history of medieval glass and its fate today.

The proportion of sand to ash is never fixed. Therefore, glass can be produced from pure sand, from pure ash or from their mixture. The decisive factor in the process is the melting point of the mixture, as the higher the proportion of sand, the higher the temperature must be. The amount of sand also determines the strength of the glass and thus its stability against corrosion. This was discovered in the Middle Ages, when in the fourteenth century the portion of ash in the glass became so high that by the fifteenth and sixteenth centuries extensive restoration became necessary.

However, the better balanced proportion of one part sand (silica) to two parts ash (alkali) was used throughout the Middle Ages, using the available melting temperature of 1200° C. This proportion would have been sufficient to preserve the windows until today with only minor corrosive defects. The destruction caused by the iconoclasts in the sixteenth and seventeenth centuries, however, forced the first major restoration campaign in Canterbury, carried out by George Austin (1819-48), and his son George Austin jnr. (1848-62), followed by Samuel Caldwell sen. (1862-1908) and Samuel Caldwell jnr. (1908-1952).

During this campaign the restoration was carried out partly by concentrating the surviving panels as stopgaps and by replacing cracked original glass and sometimes entire panels. Even if this kind of restoration can be blamed today for the repeated loss of medieval glass and its inadmissible alteration from its original connection, it has to be admitted that this restoration programme made the preservation of most of the glass only possible.

Today, however, the conservators are confronted with another problem, the decay of glass because of changes in the environment. Since the advent of heating in churches, permanent moisture in the form of condensation on the inner surface of the glass has caused akalis to be leached out. The remaining silica becomes iridescent, rendering the glass opaque. On the outer surface, the presence nowadays of sulphur dioxide in the atmosphere causes a chemical reaction with the alkali, which turns to chalk. The resultant crust, often visible on windows still to be restored, further attracts permanent moisture.

A survey of the windows of Canterbury Cathedral in 1971 showed it was obvious that the glass was in an advanced state of decay and a restoration programme was desperately needed. Thus a conservation studio was set up in the Precincts, which since then has restored the windows in a sequence according to their urgency.

The first step in the restoration is the removal of the respective window into the studio. Since the decay of every single piece of glass depends on its chemical composition and its location in the window, a decision has to be made for every panel as to how the restoration should be carried out. Due to the present day principle of preserving the original remainder,

Detail of the Corona east window *before* and *after* restoration.

the restoration is restricted to removing the dirt using soft swabs and deionised water or white spirit, whilst the weathering deposits are removed by the skilful use of glass-fibre brushes. Only in particularly serious instances will the glass be dismantled. Fragile, cracked or weakened fragments can then be strengthened by using backing plates.

Since every process in the restoration has to be reversible, no original glass is ever fired. Therefore lost paint cannot be re-stored, but details of inscriptions can be reinforced by paint applied to backing plates. Which ever of these measures are taken, every step is carefully recorded so that future conservators will be in no doubt of what has gone before.

To finish the conservation solely by re-installation of the restored windows, however, would simply start the process of the decay once again. Therefore, restoration today also includes the prevention of further deterioration by using an additional protective glazing mounted on the exterior. The space arising between both windows has to be ventilated to prevent moisture from becoming trapped.

The protective glazing has two main positive effects. It reduces hazardous elements in the atmosphere of the interface down to less than 15% and protects the inner surface of the medieval glass from condensation because of isothermals. The protective glazing could have the effect of disfiguring the architecture if it was used only as a large pane, but because the glaz-ing in Canterbury is made up of leaded lights with main leaded lines of the original the reflective area of glass is broken up and echoes the mosaic appearance of the medieval window.

Restored in this way the medieval window retains its original form and regains its former splendour. Its adequate protection enables future generations to admire the masterpieces of the Middle Ages.

DR SEBASTIAN STROBL
Director of Stained Glass Studio

The Pentecost from the Corona east window *before* **and** *after* **restoration**

Chronological Guide to the Stained Glass

The following is intended as an aid to the dating of all the windows mentioned in the text. The numbers refer to the pages.

Late Twelfth Century

West Window — Genealogical figures 20
South-West Transept — Genealogical figures 30
North Choir Aisle — Biblia Pauperum windows 32
North Choir Aisle Clerestory — Lives of St Alphege and St Dunstan 48
North-East Transept — Rose window 52

Early Thirteenth Century

West Window — Genealogical figures 20
South-West Transept — Genealogical figures 30
Trinity Chapel — Miracle windows 54
Corona — Redemption and Tree of Jesse windows 69

Late Fourteenth Century

West Window — Kings, Apostles and heraldry 20

Fifteenth Century

North-West Transept — The Royal window 26

Nineteenth Century

North Nave Aisle — Clayton and Bell window 14
Choir Clerestory — George Austin windows 14
St Gregory's Chapel — George Austin windows 14
St John's Chapel — George Austin windows 14
St Michael's Chapel — Clayton and Bell window 14
South-West Transept — Christopher Whall windows 14
South-East Transept — Rose window 14
Chapter House — East window 18

Twentieth Century

St Anselm's Chapel — Stammers window 17
St Michael's Chapel — William Wilson window 14
North-West Transept — Royal Family window 17
South-West Transept — Christopher Whall windows 14
South-East Transept — Bossanyi windows 17
Cloister — Christopher Webb window and Hugh Easton windows 17
Chapter House — West window 18